BY JANE R. DAVIS

History's very WORST

TEN TERRIBLE BATTLES

Gareth Stevens PUBLISHING

Please visit our website, www.garethstevens.com. For a free color catalog of all our high-quality books, call toll free 1-800-542-2595 or fax 1-877-542-2596.

Library of Congress Cataloging-in-Publication Data

Names: Davis, Jane R. author
Title: Ten terrible battles / Jane R. Davis.
Description: Buffalo, New York : Gareth Stevens Publishing, 2026. | Series: History's very worst | Includes index. | Audience: Grades 4-6
Identifiers: LCCN 2025002811 (print) | LCCN 2025002812 (ebook) | ISBN 9781482472592 (library binding) | ISBN 9781482472585 (paperback) | ISBN 9781482472608 (ebook)
Subjects: LCSH: Battles–History–Juvenile literature
Classification: LCC D25 .D368 2026 (print) | LCC D25 (ebook) | DDC 904/.7–dc23/eng/20250321
LC record available at https://lccn.loc.gov/2025002811
LC ebook record available at https://lccn.loc.gov/2025002812

Published in 2026 by
Gareth Stevens Publishing
2544 Clinton Street
Buffalo, NY 14224

Designer: Tanya Dellaccio Keeney
Editor: Kristen Nelson

Photo credits: Cover Noureldin mohamed salah/Shutterstock.com; pp. 4, 5, 15, 17, 18, 19, 22 Everett Collection/Shutterstock.com; p. 6 https://upload.wikimedia.org/wikipedia/commons/1/1a/The_Death_of_Paulus_Aemilius_at_the_Battle_of_Cannae_%28Yale_University_Art_Gallery_scan%29.jpg; p. 7 BearFotos/Shutterstock.com; p. 8 https://upload.wikimedia.org/wikipedia/commons/0/00/Richard_Caton_Woodville%27s_The_Battle_of_Towton.jpg; p. 9 German Vizulis/Shutterstock.com; p. 11 https://upload.wikimedia.org/wikipedia/commons/6/6c/Philip_King_of_Mount_Hope_by_Paul_Revere.jpeg; p. 12 https://upload.wikimedia.org/wikipedia/commons/b/b6/HoratioGatesByStuart.jpeg; p. 13 (top) Courtesy of The New York Public Library; p. 13 (bottom) https://upload.wikimedia.org/wikipedia/commons/8/8c/Lord_Cornwallis.jpg; p. 14 https://upload.wikimedia.org/wikipedia/commons/f/ff/Thure_de_Thulstrup_-_Battle_of_Antietam.jpg; p. 16 Courtesy of the Library of Congress; p. 21 Andreas Wolochow/Shutterstock.com; p. 23 pablofdezr/Shutterstock.com; p. 25 https://upload.wikimedia.org/wikipedia/commons/6/61/GERMAN_TROOPS_ADVANCING_PAST_ABANDONED_AMERICAN_EQUIPMENT.jpg;p. 26 Peter Hermes Furian/Shutterstock.com; p. 27 https://upload.wikimedia.org/wikipedia/commons/6/61/GERMAN_TROOPS_ADVANCING_PAST_ABANDONED_AMERICAN_EQUIPMENT.jpg;p. 29 Courtesy of TommyJapan1/Flickr.com.

Printed in the United States of America

CPSIA compliance information: Batch #CSGS26 For further information contact Gareth Stevens,at 1-800-542-2595.

CONTENTS

Words in the glossary appear in **bold** the first time they are used in the text.

GOING TO BATTLE

A battle is a meeting of opposing military forces. At times in history, battles were fought by huge armies with swords and shields. As weapons improved, armies came to use guns, tanks, and bombs—all of which led to some of the worst battles of all time.

In history, soldiers on one side of a battle could tell which other soldiers were the enemy by their uniform. The sides are less clear in modern battles.

From ancient times to the Vietnam War, people have fought in increasingly terrible battles. Some had hundreds of thousands of casualties. Many were just one battle in a larger war. Why did these battles happen? And was their outcome worth the human cost? Read on and decide for yourself!

THE UGLY TRUTH

CASUALTIES ARE THE SOLDIERS AND CIVILIANS, OR NON-SOLDIERS, THAT DIE, ARE HURT, OR BECOME SICK DURING A WAR OR BATTLE.

THE BATTLE OF CANNAE

The Republic of Rome and the African city of Carthage fought three wars against one another from 264 to 164 BCE. One of the bloodiest battles of these wars occurred near the town of Cannae on August 2, 216 BCE.

The three wars between the Roman Republic and Carthage are now called the Punic Wars.

RUINS OF CARTHAGE

THE UGLY TRUTH

ONLY A FEW ROMAN SOLDIERS ESCAPED. THOSE WHO WEREN'T KILLED WERE TAKEN PRISONER BY CARTHAGE.

Carthage set up its forces in an arc with the weakest forces pushed forward in the center. When the Romans attacked, they believed themselves to be winning as they easily took down these soldiers. But the Romans were actually fighting their way deeper into Carthage's best forces, and they were soon **surrounded**. About 50,000 to 70,000 Roman soldiers were killed over the course of the next few hours.

BATTLE OF TOWTON

In the mid- to late 1400s, both the families of the Yorks and the Lancasters believed they had the right to the English throne. The battles between them are known as the Wars of the Roses. The Battle of Towton during this conflict was one of the bloodiest ever to occur on English soil.

THE UGLY TRUTH

SO MANY OF THE LANCASTER FORCES WERE KILLED AT THE BATTLE OF TOWTON—AS MANY AS 28,000—THAT THE LANCASTERS COULDN'T FIELD AN ARMY FOR THREE YEARS!

A few months after the Battle of Towton, Edward IV—a York—became king of England.

York and Lancaster forces met in a snowstorm near a village called Towton on March 29, 1461. They fought for 10 hours without either side gaining the advantage. Then, more troops arrived to help York forces. The Lancaster soldiers ran for it—and many were killed as they fled.

A Final Battle

By the late 1600s, many European colonists had settled in the northeastern part of North America. However, Native American peoples, including the Wampanoag, had been living there for thousands of years. They wanted to stop the settlers from taking their land.

Metacom, chief of the Wampanoag, gathered a group of Native Americans to fight the settlers. Fighting started in 1675. The Native Americans attacked and killed settlers and ruined their homes.

The Ugly Truth

About 3,000 Native Americans died during King Philip's War.

This conflict is called King Philip's War today. The English called Metacom, shown here, King Philip. His death on August 12, 1676, led to the end of the war.

Colonial troops fought back, resulting in **devastating** losses for the Native Americans. The last true battle of the war occurred at Mount Hope in Rhode Island. Metacom was killed in the battle. Then, he was beheaded.

The Battle of Camden

By 1780, the new United States had been fighting Great Britain for its freedom for five years. The southern forces of the Continental, or American, army had little proper food. Most of the soldiers had little experience and training. Many were ill as they marched to Camden, South Carolina, in August 1780. They met British forces on their way.

The Continental forces in the Battle of Camden were led by General Horatio Gates. He was removed from his post after this **defeat**—which only took about an hour!

THE UGLY TRUTH

THE BATTLE OF CAMDEN IS REMEMBERED AS ONE OF THE WORST LOSSES IN THE HISTORY OF THE AMERICAN MILITARY.

CHARLES CORNWALLIS

On August 16, the two armies met on a forested battlefield. As the British advanced, as many as 2,000 American soldiers ran away! The British general Charles Cornwallis directed the British **cavalry** to fight through the Americans who were left.

THE BATTLE OF ANTIETAM

The United States fought a bloody civil war from 1861 to 1865. Eleven southern states had **seceded** from the Union mostly over the issue of slavery.

THE UGLY TRUTH

THE BATTLE OF ANTIETAM WAS ONE OF THE BLOODIEST OF THE WAR. CONFEDERATE TROOPS LOST MORE THAN 10,000 SOLDIERS. THE UNITED STATES HAD CASUALTIES NUMBERING OVER 12,000.

General Lee wanted to **invade** the North. However, the Battle of Antietam pushed his Confederate forces back into Virginia. The United States called this a victory.

Confederate, or southern, forces, led by General Robert E. Lee, met United States troops near Antietam Creek in Maryland on September 17, 1862. Led by General George B. McClellan, the Union soldiers attacked the Confederates on a battlefield now called the Cornfield. Casualties were high, but fighting continued on a nearby road.

Union Major General Ambrose Burnside was able to push Confederate troops back enough to cross the creek. However, fresh Confederate troops arrived. U.S. troops had to retreat, or fall back.

The Battle of Gettysburg

In 1863, General Lee was again trying to invade the North. He led his troops into Pennsylvania. U.S. forces were waiting near the town of Gettysburg. The two sides fought from July 1 to July 3.

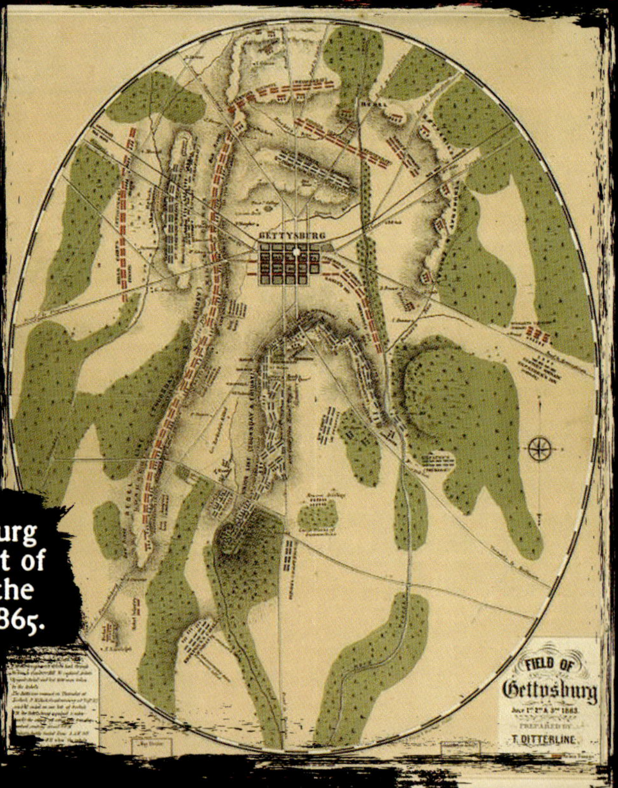

The Battle of Gettysburg is called a turning point of the Civil War, which the United States won in 1865.

THE UGLY TRUTH

BOTH ARMIES FACED HIGH CASUALTIES IN THE BATTLE OF GETTYSBURG. THERE WAS A TOTAL OF ABOUT 46,000 TO 51,000 CASUALTIES.

On the first day, there were more Confederate soldiers than U.S. soldiers, and the U.S. forces got pushed back. By the second day, there were 94,000 U.S. soldiers to the Confederate army's 72,000. Many soldiers were lost on both sides in the fighting. On the third day, Confederate general Charles George Pickett attacked the U.S. troops head on. This failed and the Confederate army retreated.

THE BATTLE OF SOMME

During **World War I**, French and British forces planned an attack on German troops near Somme, France, in June 1916.

THE UGLY TRUTH

THE FIRST AMERICAN DEATH OF THE WAR OCCURRED DURING THE BATTLE OF SOMME. THE SOLDIER HARRY BUTTERS WAS AN AMERICAN SERVING WITH BRITISH FORCES.

Trench warfare was used throughout World War I, including during the Battle of Somme. Soldiers on both sides dug trenches to hide in and fire from.

The British began by **shelling** the Germans for a week. However, half the shells didn't detonate, or explode, and few Germans were harmed. When the British finally attacked on foot, they found German troops in **trenches** behind **barbed** wire. On July 1 alone, 57,000 British soldiers were killed.

The British didn't give up. Both sides used all the modern firepower they had available. The British even brought out the first tanks. After the 141-day battle, there were more than 1 million casualties total.

World War II

World War II was fought from 1939 to 1945. It was a conflict between two sets of countries, the Allied Powers (or Allies) and the Axis Powers (or Axis). In 1933, Adolf Hitler had risen to power in Germany. The country had been treated harshly in the treaty that ended World War I. Its economy suffered. Hitler and the political party he led, the Nazi Party, gave Germans hope for a better future.

Allies	Axis
Great Britain	Germany
France	Italy
Russia	Japan
China	
United States	

Hitler (center) called himself the *Führer*, or leader with total power, of Germany.

THE UGLY TRUTH

THE NAZIS PUT PEOPLE IN PRISON CAMPS, OR CONCENTRATION CAMPS, TO FACE **STARVATION** AND DEATH. THEY **TARGETED** JEWISH PEOPLE, AMONG OTHER GROUPS.

However, Hitler was willing to do great **violence** to get what he wanted. And he wanted Germany to take over Europe. When Germany invaded Poland in 1939, Great Britain and France declared war.

The Battle of Stalingrad

Hitler began trying to invade the Soviet Union in the summer of 1942. At first, the invasion went well and the German forces were ready to take the city of Stalingrad. They bombed the city into a ruin.

THE UGLY TRUTH

THE LEADER OF SOVIET UNION, JOSEPH STALIN, WOULDN'T LET THE CITY NAMED FOR HIM GO EASILY. EVERY SOLDIER AND CIVILIAN WAS MADE TO DO SOMETHING TO HELP SAVE THE CITY.

Stalingrad was on a major river in the Soviet Union, a country in eastern Europe and northern Asia that existed from 1922 to 1991. It included present-day Russia, Lithuania, and Latvia, among others.

For months, Soviet and German soldiers fought in the destroyed streets of Stalingrad. Germany neared a victory. Then, in November 1942, Soviet troops surrounded Stalingrad, trapping the Germans inside. But the Germans didn't give up until February 1943!

It was a terrible loss of life. About 500,000 German soldiers died in the Battle of Stalingrad. More than 1 million Soviet soldiers were killed—as well as 40,000 civilians.

The Battle of the Bulge

By 1944, the United States was a major part of the Allied forces in World War II. In December of that year, Hitler directed German forces to the Ardennes Forest in the European countries of Belgium and Luxembourg. They took the Allies, including U.S. troops, by surprise.

British and U.S. forces kept the Germans back long enough for more Allied troops to arrive. The Germans were only able to make a "bulge" in the defense lines of the Allies. By January 1945, U.S. forces had pushed the Germans back.

Though the Americans helped win this battle, about 19,000 U.S. Army soldiers died.

The Battle of the Bulge was the deadliest battle for U.S. forces in World War II.

THE UGLY TRUTH

GERMAN CASUALTIES NUMBERED ANYWHERE FROM 80,000 TO 100,000. THE LOSS HIT THE GERMAN FORCES HARD. A GERMAN DEFEAT CAME JUST FIVE MONTHS LATER IN MAY 1945.

VIETNAM: THE BATTLE OF HUE

In 1954, the Asian country of Vietnam broke apart into North Vietnam and South Vietnam. North Vietnam wanted the country to come back together under Communism. South Vietnam wanted to remain separate. Fighting between the two parts of Vietnam started by 1957.

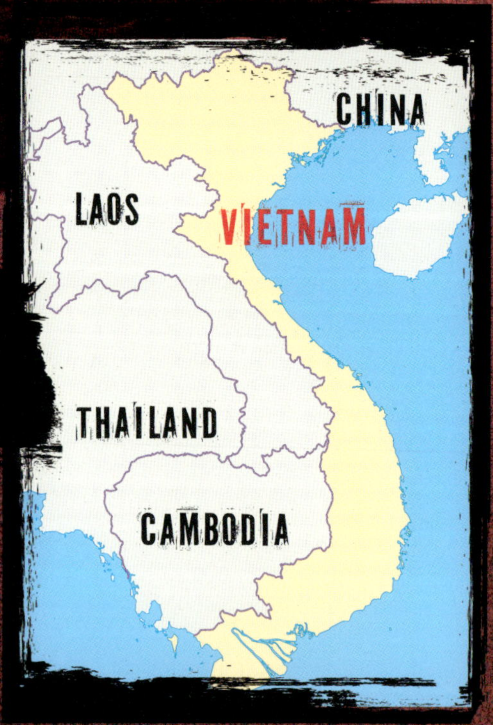

The United States supported South Vietnam because the U.S. government didn't like Communism.

THE UGLY TRUTH

COMMUNISM IS A POLITICAL AND ECONOMIC SYSTEM IN WHICH THERE IS ONE POLITICAL PARTY THAT LEADS A COUNTRY. IT CONTROLS HOW AND WHAT GOODS ARE MADE IN THE COUNTRY.

In 1964, an attack on a U.S. ship in the Gulf of Tonkin by North Vietnamese fighters convinced leaders in the United States to become even more involved in the war. By 1968, more than 500,000 American soldiers were serving in Vietnam.

In January 1968, North Vietnamese troops attacked the city of Hue. U.S. and South Vietnamese forces fought them in the streets and homes of the city.

The battle continued in this way for a month. The U.S. forces weren't used to fighting in a city and found it difficult. North Vietnamese supporters called the Viet Kong captured and killed thousands of civilians. The city of Hue was destroyed so completely that about 100,000 people were left without homes. About half of the U.S. Marines fighting in the Battle of Hue were killed.

In 1975, North Vietnam invaded South Vietnam and reunited the country. Twenty years later, the Vietnamese government reported that about 2 million civilians died in the war. As many as 1.3 million Vietnamese soldiers on both sides also died.

THE UGLY TRUTH

SINCE THE VIETNAM WAR, THE UNITED STATES HAS BEEN PART OF WAR IN THE MIDDLE EAST, INCLUDING IN AFGHANISTAN, IRAQ, AND SYRIA, AS WELL AS IN PARTS OF AFRICA.

The Battle of Hue was one battle in a larger part of the Vietnam War called the Tet Offensive. Tet is a Vietnamese holiday.

GLOSSARY

barbed: Having a barb, or a sharp point that bends backward and isn't easy to remove.

cavalry: The part of the army made up of soldiers trained to fight on horseback.

defeat: To beat.

devastating: Causing widespread damage.

invade: To enter a place to take it over.

secede: To leave a country.

shell: To throw shells at. A shell is something shot out of a gun or cannon that explodes.

surround: To enclose on all sides.

starvation: The state of dying from hunger.

target: The focus of effort.

trench: A long, narrow hole dug in the ground.

violence: The use of force to harm someone.

World War I: A war fought from 1914 to 1918 that involved countries from around the world.

FOR MORE INFORMATION

BOOKS

Hama, Larry, et. al. *World War II Battles*. Buffalo, NY; Rosen Publishing, 2024.

Ventura, Marne. *12 Iconic American Battles*. Mankato, MN: Black Rabbit Books, 2025.

Yenne, Bill. *100 Events That Shaped World History*. Naperville, IL: Sourcebooks Explore, 2022.

WEBSITES

Answers to Questions Kids Ask About the Revolutionary War
https://www.battlefields.org/learn/articles/answers-questions-kids-ask-about-revolutionary-war
Find out more about the American Revolution through these questions and answers.

10 Facts About World War 2
https://www.natgeokids.com/uk/discover/history/general-history/world-war-two/
Get more information about the Second World War here.

INDEX